Simon Startin

Simon Startin has worked as a professional theatre-maker since 1991. Initially as an actor, working with such companies as Graeae, Royal Exchange Manchester, Hampstead Theatre, Red Shift and Fittings, as well as roles on film and television. In 2002 he branched into writing through the Paines Plough "Wild Lunch" scheme. The resulting play *Revolting* was funded by London Arts and premiered at the Xposure Festival, a dark satire on models of disability telling the story of "Happenstance" – the cripple Christ never cured.

Since then he has struck up a fruitful relationship with London Bubble Theatre Company, writing nine pieces for them, five of which were awarded the *Time Out* Critics' Choice.

His other plays include: *The Crock of Gold, Myths, Rituals* and *Whitegoods, Metamorphoses, Odyssey, Mezzanine* and *Sirens of Titan.*

Currently, Simon is Co-creative Director of the The Big Lounge Collective, a production company that promotes the work of emerging disabled artists.

His play *Blackbirds,* produced by London Bubble, is also published by Aurora Metro Books.

First published in the UK in 2013 by Aurora Metro Publications Ltd

67 Grove Avenue, Twickenham, TW1 4HX

www.aurorametro.com info@aurorametro.com

From Docks to Desktops © 2013 Simon Startin

Cover design © Emmi design

Production: Simon Smith

With many thanks to: Anna Laura Festa, Fay Allum, Molly Gibbons, Neil Gregory, Richard Turk, Alex Chambers.

10 9 8 7 6 5 4 3 2 1

Printed by imprintdigital.com, Exeter, UK

ISBN: 978-1-906582-54-8

FROM DOCKS
TO DESKTOPS

Inspired by

South Londoners

Developed by

Jonathan Petherbridge

Written by

SIMON STARTIN

AURORA METRO BOOKS

London Bubble would like to thank:

The story tellers: Barbara Acheampong, Jim Annand, Margaret Aspey, Ike Bakers, Betty Baldry, Mark Bean, John Byran, David Clark, Chris Carr, Len Dawes, Hazel Dixon, Vanessa Dowling, Bert Drane, Joan Drane, Patrick Doyle, Barry Albin Dyer, Kitty Finch, Dave Fisher, Izzet Gocer, Len Hatch, Sylvie Honeyman, Jane Jeffery, Pat Jenkins, Lee Kempster, Dave Kershaw, Patrick Kingwell, Danny Lavelle, Frank Long, Dave Morrison, Ada Newman, Ida Paul, Hasit Patel, John Penver, Helen Penver, Mick Reardon, Michael Reardon, Linda Rider, Mary Ripper, Dorothy Sinclair, Fred Stone, Irene Thomas, John Tyler, Maureen Tyson, Doug Wainwright, June Wainwright, Brenda Watkinson, Stephen William.

The story gatherers: Philippa Acton, Judith Arkwright, Jasmine Atkinson, Shaun Barrett, Sally Caulker, Simon Cole, Sara Cook, Nina Dawson, Jas Dhell, Amanda Devoir, Edward Garlick, Deshaye Gayle, Catriona Hay, Chris Holland, Olivia Lamont, Kemi Lofinmakin, Ian MacNaughton, Ariane Mak, Lauren Maile-Wilson, Jodie Witcher, Tamara Noble, Lisa O'Brien, Rosy Rickett, Michele Winter, Megan Vine, Anuska Zaremba-Pike.

Volunteers: Jane Annand, Charlotte Bell, Tia Blake, Barbara Braithwaite, John Breacher, Matea Brezec, Natasha Brisden, Jessica Earls, Gloria Emmanuel, Iris Dove, Caitlin Kennedy, Sophia Moss, Stephan Nahring, Juliet Nelson, Gill Newton, Patrick Olliffe, Conor Parker, Jack Palmer, Rachael Pooley, Stephen Teelan, Patrick Olliffe, Sue Sexton.

Thanks also to:

Our supporters: The Heritage Lottery Fund, The Arts Council England, Rotherhithe Community Council, and the Esmée Fairbairn Foundation.

Our thanks also go to Gary Magold, and the staff at Southwark Local History library.

CONTENTS

FOREWORD

This script is one outcome of a rich process involving community volunteers, professional artists and a local theatre company. Nearly two hundred people were involved in what London Bubble calls 'Foraging', a process of gathering material – testimony, images, statistics, artefacts and muscle memories. Once gathered, this wealth of material was sorted, or 'Prepped' in exploratory workshops involving anyone who wanted to join in with the theatre-making. So over five months, fifty people attended fifteen workshops which examined the testimony and images to focus the material and create suggestions as to how it might be used. They created rough scenes, made sequences of patterned movement, looked at how recorded interview material might be used and tried characters – some of which worked, some of which didn't.

Towards the end of this process, the company was joined by writer Simon Startin, designer Pip Nash and sound artist Ben Hauke, and these three specialists then started their work shaping the prepped material. The three took the ideas away and used their specialist skills to produce a 'Recipe' using the ingredients – a script, design and soundscape. But in order to maintain shared ownership, these were then offered up for consideration and feedback from the wider group. Comments were made and informed subsequent drafts. Thereafter, the process was much like any other show, as the hard work of rehearsals began, involving a core cast of thirty, ranging in age between 9 and 80+. After the first half of the piece had been rehearsed the people who had originally donated and gathered the raw material were invited to a scratch, script-in-hand sharing, and asked to give their feedback.

I've started to call this genre *vernacular theatre*. 'Vernacular architecture' is defined as 'based on localised needs and construction materials and reflecting local traditions'. Vernacular theatre is similarly hewn from local material and shaped by local knowledge (all our artists are also embedded in South East London). Like the process of raising a barn, this sort of theatre-making is a social process involving all ages and having its own particular aesthetic. I believe it helps strengthen community connections, passes knowledge between generations and brings much joy.

Jonathan Petherbridge

Creative Director, London Bubble

INTRODUCTION

Verbatim theatre has a voguish currency at the moment, which makes me simultaneously intrigued and suspicious. It makes a claim for authenticity. It is 'real voices' deployed to tell the 'truth'. In the hundreds of hours of interviews recorded for this project, good people told their stories with honesty and integrity, communicating vividly the truth of their experience of work and life within Bermondsey for the last eighty or so years. However, in the curation of their voices into a theatre piece, there is a duty to both reflect the myriad of individual stories told and to present a wider view. This bigger picture starts to move away from the authenticity of an individual voice towards an overarching message to be communicated, and is open to bias. Nevertheless, whilst recognising that there is no such thing as a neutral selection in verbatim work, I have tried to remain true to the sense within the interviews of Bermondsey having an incredibly turbulent time of it under the great tidal wave of globalisation. I make no bones of my belief that decisions made in far-flung corridors of power and global corporations have placed Bermondsey under great stress, ripping through the cohesion and livelihoods of the community, when capitalism turns predatory at the expense of humanity. So I have endeavoured to allow these voices to speak as tribute to the survival of hard-working people in the face of greed and power. Moreover, I have tried to express the current unease felt by many today as to the future of work, as capital not only recedes from Bermondsey but from the UK as a whole, and we are left to ponder what we truly value and the sacrifices we are willing to make to defend it.

Simon Startin

FROM DOCKS TO DESKTOPS

SIMON STARTIN

A London Bubble Theatre production, which opened on 15th November 2013.

London Bubble Core Staff

Mike Adam
Finance Officer

Lucy Anderson Jones
Fundraiser and Development Manager

Adam Annand
Associate Director, Creative Learning

Lucy Bradshaw
Administrator

Sagan Daniels
LB+ Promoter

Shipra Ogra
Producer

Jonathan Petherbridge
Creative Director

Claire Sexton
Project Coordinator (Inter-generational Projects)

Marie Vickers
Project Leader LB+

Board of Directors

Pat Abraham, Jonathan Barnes, Jocelyn Cunningham, Matthew De Lange, Mark Dunford, Charlie Folorunsho, Simon Hughes MP, June Mitchell, Francisco Mojica, David Slater, Wendy Stone, Sue Timothy, Simon Thomson

Creative Team

Jonathan Petherbridge
Project Director

Simon Startin
Writer

Julia Voce
Company Director

Pip Nash
Set and Costume Designer

Fraz Roughton
Costume Supervisor

Ben Hauke
Sound Designer

Nao Ngai
Lighting Designer

Vicky O'Neill
Stage Manager

Michael Breakey
Constructor

Francis Watson
Frame Maker

Cast

Philippa Acton

Judith Arkwright

Jasmine Atkinson

Lucy Bradshaw

Catherine Davis

Iris Dove

Vanessa Dowling

Jessica Earls

Emelia Findlay

Chris Hawney

Rosy Lea Hawney

Robert Herzog

Kezia Herzog

Chris Holland

Asya Karababa

Hacer Karababa

Ian MacNaughton

Eamon Martin

Patrick Olliffe

Lee Philips

Wendy Ponting

Muhammed Salim

Alex Saoutkin

Omar Shehata

Andrew Stern

Jane Tilton

Maureen Tyson

Brenda Watkinson

Ken Woolhouse

London Bubble Theatre Company

5 Elephant Lane,

London SE16 4JD

admin@londonbubble.org.uk

www.londonbubble.org.uk

Registered Charity No: 264 359

VAT Registration: 240 1591 96

Company Registration: 1058397

London Bubble Theatre Company are grateful for
financial assistance from the Heritage Lottery Fund, the
Arts Council England, Esmée Fairbairn Foundation and
Bermondsey and Rotherhithe Community Council

FROM DOCKS
TO DESKTOPS

Dedicated to the memory of Len Hatch

FROM DOCKS TO DESKTOPS

A child on an empty stage.

CHILD   My hands. My ears. My eyes.
                 My face. My smile. My suffering.
                 My judgment. My knowledge. My
                 Skills. My strength. My courage. My
                 luck. My time. My life. My labour.

The child lays out chairs in the space, and is joined by a chorus of interviewers with recording equipment, which they prepare.

LUCY   One... two... one... two...

JAS   This is Jas... this is Jas...

JESSICA   My name is Jessica.

ALEX   One... two...

ASYA   I'm Amanda Devoir.

LUCY   One... two..

ASYA   Devoir... Devoir...

A chorus of interviewees sit in their respective chairs, some helped by assistants. They get themselves comfortable. Cups of tea are brought. Cushions are plumped.

JOAN   Bert? Bert?!

BERT   What?

JOAN   They're 'ere!

BERT   What?

JOAN   Bubble!

BERT	Who?
JOAN	Bubble!
BERT	Oh gawd.
ASYA	I'm Amanda Devoir, I'm with John in his house.
KEZIA	Okay, so my name is Sarah, and I'm here with Dave in his house...
ANON 2	I was born in Bermondsey, in London, and I was born in 1950.
ADA	I was born on the 5th of the 12 1919. I shall be 93 this December.
VANESSA	1946.
BETTY	1932.
MIKE	Pardon?
KATRINA	Can you tell us about your work please?

Pause

PAT M	Pardon?
KEZIA	Can you tell us a little bit about your work?

An old-fashioned tape player plays on stage. The chorus gather round the player, straining to hear the recording of the voices.

MICK	I can't flipping remember...
MARY	I'm thinking – I'm thinking, let me think dates. Erm...
MICK	She used to be good with dates, but since she had this...

JESSICA	Can't quite...
MARY	So that would have been, yeah, that would have been about seventy three, seventy four. Your first time there.
ALEX	Difficult...
MICK	I even used to run up there.
ASYA	Distant...
MARY	Then you went back in, Michael's seventy-nine... eighty-one.
MICK	Yeah another few years.
MARY	And you were there for about fourteen years.
MICK	Quite a long time.
CHORUS	Quite a long time.
MARY	No, eighty-one.

The cast talk to the audience (*** = point of overlap)

JANE	I worked as a cook, cleaner, ***aromatherapist and massage practitioner, reflexologist, event organiser, administrator, receptionist, manager, bar worker, recruitment officer, teacher of massage, reading helper, waitress, fundraiser.
LUCY	I worked as a shop assistant, a post sorter, ***a cinema usher, a theatre usher, a youth theatre assistant, a box office assistant, an outreach administrator, a receptionist, a team secretary, a BSF bid

coordinator, an audience development manager, a theatre administrator.

MAUREEN   I worked in a tax office, in Harrods books department, ***as a hospital orderly, a cook, a pea packer, mail sorter, barista, a market researcher, mother and political campaigner.

WENDY   I worked as a production manager, ***office manager, receptionist, runner, phone-in assistant, box office assistant, waitress, bar maid, shop worker and stage manager.

CHRIS HOL   I've been a van driver's assistant, ***a gardener, a clerical assistant, a waste disposal operative, installed antique fireplaces, a waiter, a shop assistant, an accounts assistant and in a press office.

JUDITH   In the last ten years I've worked as a teacher, ***office worker, community worker, cook, mother, manager, counsellor, carer for aging relatives.

PHILIPPA   A secondary school teacher of English, ***a teacher of drama, of art, PHSE and citizenship. As a librarian, a secretary, a television researcher, food-packer and waitress.

IRIS   I've worked as a primary school teacher, ***Open University tutor, volunteer archivist and researcher, ecology park volunteer, tour guide, cat socializer, and performer.

ANDREW   I've worked as a local government communications officer, singer, community mediator, ***refurbisher of a holiday home, community theatre maker and carer.

KEN   I've worked as a chaplain, a prison visitor, ***a befriender, a support carer and grandchild minder.

CATHERINE   mother, actor, teacher, ***workshop leader, museum animator.

IAN   I've been a teacher as well, a van driver, handout man, ***actor, census official.

ROBERT   I worked as a cycle courier, ***a single parent, a boyfriend/lover.

MUHAMMED   A general warehouse assistant ***and a business admin assistant.

BRENDA   I set up my own freelance typing and secretarial service.

A school room.

JOHN B   See the school, St Michael's School where I went, and St Joseph's, the primary school was right on the edge of the dock. We were surrounded on three sides with wharfs and the river. So, you'd look out your classroom and see the cranes moving. There's not one time any teacher or anyone ever said anything to us about going to university. It was always do well at school and you could be a bricklayer. Do well at school and you could be an electrician.

KITTY
I was desperate to go where there was lots and lots of people that's what it said on my School Certificate. It said she wants to go where there are lots of people, she's this lovely bubbly girl.

SPEED
We were only educated for factory fodder.

PAT D
I left school in Croydon Road, partially deaf. School was hard for me because I couldn't hear. One evening he came home from the pub and he said 'I may have a chance for you to get an apprenticeship.' I went for an interview and I got the job.

LEN D
My father worked as a stevedore in the Surrey Commercial Docks. At that particular time, the only way you could work there was to be a member of the union. And the only way you could be a member of the union was if you had a direct blood relative that worked in the docks. My father said, I'll get you in the docks.

ANON 2
We never had no money. There was lots of things like, my dad going on strikes if it was like a week where there was no money and I remember going to work in a pair of, em, hush puppies with long socks. And I felt horrible, really horrible, 'cos you wanted to be grown-up. And then on my first week's wages, which got paid in a little brown envelope, erm I got my first pair of stockings.

Ropes are pulled across.

DAVID C   I had rheumatic fever and I went to a special school which taught you a trade. I was trained in the college in bespoke shoemaking, which was handmade shoes. I went to a place called Master's which was making surgical shoes for different deformities.

A rope walkway is held by the cast and the young Irene crosses.

IRENE   I won a trade scholarship, but I couldn't do anything 'cos my mother's got – my mother had six children. I was the eldest, so she wanted me to come back to London 'cos she needed the money. My mother took me to Peek Frean's.

Sounds of the conveyor belt.

ADA   The biscuit factory. Drummond Road.

IRENE   At one time everybody worked at Peek Frean's. There was 4,000 workers there when I first started. And I loved it there. I loved it there. I only used to have to cross the road and go into work.

SYLVIE   Had to be fast, had to collect all what was comin' down the belt and you'd have three teams of eight, they'd all be packin' 'em, the packets, and they'd come down the belt and your job was to take every one of 'em, you couldn't move from the machine because the biscuits

	would go in the machine and crush up, all crush up.
ADA	You'd have your biscuits by the side of you, as it's coming along, you if was a mixed one, and you'd have to biscuit where it's supposed to be.
SYLVIE	I first of all started in, new building as called MB1, just ordinary making up. Then I got promoted to MB2, export. But it was 'ard 'ard 'arder work, there was er tins where you had to put all the assorted biscuits in and put corrugated paper all round 'em you used to use all your hand nails, every finger was done up with a bit of tape but you dun it.
IRENE	They'd keep the belts going so many girls would go off the belt and somebody would go on 'cos the law says you gotta have a break, innit.
SYLVIE	If they had no work you used to have to go up on the puddin' floor, oh, Christmas puddin' floor, you had it all over you – like cause you had to scoop the tops to make 'em flat in the basins and it'd be all over ya. I didn't like that.
IRENE	People used to make me laugh, 'Oh I like Marks and Spencer puddings', but they weren't Marks and Spencer puddings, they were ours.
CHRIS C	There was a little ritual up in the pudding plant. There was a table with a white ironed table cloth, and a nice

bowl, and a silver spoon, and every day I tasted the christmas pud and I signed the book. You can measure everything; density, humidity, fruit content, but ultimately what do people do? They eat the bloody thing.

ADA I used like being on the Christmas puddings. They'd come along and just warm. She'd go like 'Oh god! I dropped the basin! I dropped the Christmas Pudding!'

Sound fades as pudding is swept up – the girls stop working and nibble biscuits.

IRENE Oh you could smell the puddings. They were made all year round and when they was on Cheeselets you'd smell the Cheeselets, and then when they was on Twiglets you'd smell the Marmite.

CHRIS C I can tell you the dimensions of a Bourbon Biscuit, just by holding it in hand. It's in the DNA.

ADA I got a three day suspension for eating a custard cream.

The girls cough up crumbs.

SPEED Cross & Blackwell's in Crimscott Street terrible job really, looking back it was in what we called the hot rooms. Sweat used to pour off us. Eight in the morning, half past six at night, Friday's six o'clock.

Sound and work changes.

VANESSA   I worked in a Bird's Eye factory. I was there mainly for the green beans.

Sound and work changes.

BETTY   I was drilling out the barrels of pens before they went to be polished and assembled. You just held the drill and sort of went in and out. Sometimes they used to break and I'd get cuts on fingers, so I used to wrap some bandage or plasters round my fingers.

Sound and work changes.

LINDA   Ice cream factory, that's another one. Yeah, Lyons Maid. I was supervisor there and was funny because Nonny, who was the boss, she wore a red turban. You had all white clothes, white boots and everything else. These jobs comes up, she puts my name on it. 'Who's put my name on here? I didn't put my name on here.' So she went 'I have.' I said, 'What for? I don't want to be a charge hand.' She said, 'You've got it, haven't you?' 'What's that?' she says – 'Without no hesitation these women will work for you.' You said to them, "Come on girls let's go, let's get this job done." I heard you.'

Whistle signals tea-break.

IRENE   I knew I had to go to work we all had to go to work, years ago if you didn't work you was lazy. Everybody worked didn't they?

ADA   I can remember my mum's face, 'They gave you three days off because you ate a custard cream?!'

The girls blow out crumbs. Sweeping.

David Clark's shoe workshop. He is preparing the leather.

DAVID C   You have to mould it, you have to make it mellow by wetting it, then as it dries out, you're also actually shaping it to size and skiving it down, to thin, to nothing at the edges. I often used to go out to buy up leathers from the wholesalers. You're handling them you know, you can tell by shaking them and also by feel. You know exactly what you want because the different parts of the animal have all got different... the belly... is a different. Different parts of the cow are all used for different parts of the shoemaking. So you have to know exactly what you're buying. When you just see plain, in like handbags, it's mainly younger animals, it's not cow, it's either calf... so it's younger skins. So you have to know. You know this by the handling.

The cast talk to the audience again.

BRENDA   I either worked from home, or at my clients' houses. ***And they dictated their books or screenplays, or their theatre plays.

MUHAMMED In the warehouse I collected health and beauty products into plastic totes in wheelie cages ***for delivery by lorries. It was part time manual labour. much like dock work I suppose.

ROBERT As a cycle courier I cycle round central London ***picking up letters/packages from clients and delivering them to another address in London. I get paid for the number of jobs I do per day.

IAN As a van driver I delivered leaflet, pamphlets ***flyers and other publicity, all over London.

CATHERINE A museum animateur.***

KEN One day a month I was on duty in the Cathedral from 10.30 until 4.30. After leading brief prayers every hour ***the Duty Chaplain announces 'Thank you for joining me in our prayers. I am available if you would like to speak to me on a spiritual matter.'

ANDREW Making community theatre brings no financial reward. ***The sense of freedom that it brings me through taking part is all the greater because of that.

IRIS I met students, devised ice-breakers, devised learning activities to promote learning ***and working together, gave guidance on essay writing, marked essays, socialised. It involved brain work, typing, sitting, moving around rooms and London.

PHILIPPA   As a drama teacher...

JUDITH   Being a mother and cook involves growing some of the food, planning meals for a whole week, shopping for the meals ***researching recipes, time management skills, chopping skills, batch cooking for freezing or to take meals to aging relatives, liaising with partners' children, inviting guests for roasts on Sundays, washing up, managing others to do the washing up.

CHRIS   As a refuse disposal operative I had to be at work by 5.30 in the morning ***collect discarded furniture from abandoned council houses and flats, and then recycle it.

WENDY   As a bar maid ***I worked in a hotel, behind the bar for weddings, or in a marquee, serving champagne, serving food, teas and coffees, washing glasses, cleaning tables, taking money.

MAUREEN   Hot dusting, wash down beds, lockers, window sills. Clear, sterilise, fumigate cupboard and wash bed pans. Break. Serve mid morning drinks, ***tidy kitchen, check fire in range, prepare lunch trolley. Help sister serve lunches, help patients, collect dishes and cutlery. Wash up. Break for lunch. Prepare tea, slice bread, collect eggs for patients, serve tea, wash up, check kitchen. Home.

LUCY   I had a desk in the main reception of an arts centre. I used a computer and sold tickets for performances and workshops over the phone and to people who arrived in person. ***Sometimes it was very very quiet and I wouldn't sell many tickets in a shift. I would work for about 4 hours in a shift. Sometimes daytimes and sometimes evenings.

JANE   I provided a full body massage with essential oils, massaged all sorts of people, old, young, sick, healthy, children, adults. Mixed up oils for individuals to use at home, in the bath or when feeling down.

Sound of ships horn The docks. Gulls.

Recorded section.

JOHN T   You could always smell tea. Um... oil, from the ships–

JOHN B   One old fella there, Fred, he was one of those old boys what worked in the boiler. Liked to liked to drink, er, he-he-he told me once, how he go in, he was on the Somme, survived the Somme.

LEN D   The men were often a little bit short-tempered, fierce.

LEN H   I was in the barge workin' with a man that was 74 year old, simply because there was no pensions and that and he was a seaman and the dock was busy then and they just, believe me he taught me a lot, and he was the one that said to me, 'Boy you've come into the dock, if you find a good guvnor, kill 'im before he 'comes a bad one'.

The stevedores unload the cargo at the double. Their movements are gracefully competent, despite it being extremely hard work.

LEN H   It was 'ard work sometimes, you didn't have time to bleedin' moan. Load the board, board up usually it was goin' shore as it was thirty-odd on board, board lifts up, 2, 4, hooks up or eyes at the end of each board and er 2, you split into two pairs or pairs, so there was six pairs, on fruit usually there was eight pairs down the 'ole so you had each pair and you had to, you had to fill, it was usually *(pause)* six, fives, thirty each side and, er, *(pause)* that was that and fruit was the same y'know. Though you was twelve, sometimes when you was doin' dates, you only had four down the 'oles, you lost your two, four outsiders, two of them came down the 'ole, then the other two had to wait.

LEN D   A stevedore is a specialist that loads and unloads ships Dockers worked round the docks as a whole. Lightermen were in charge of the barges.

JOHN B   The cheese and the butter. Polish bacon in the boat. Sometimes they would bring in absolute rubbish. Like coat hangers, I remember standin' around looking at, they they was unloadin' coat hangers.

LEN H   You get the dates, round the Mediterranean, dates, figs and everythin' like that and the Persian gold barley and then you might get the Canadian wheat come over and everythin' like that. So it was basically most then – most then–, not 'ow it is now, most of it was just seasonal and then get the fruit, Spanish tomatoes and everythin', we used to do that, it was a lovely job that, tomatoes, money, money, money.

LEN D   I worked mostly on timber, which meant packing up long legs of timber against short legs and keeping the thicknesses together. It was a cross between playing tennis and chess. It was 100% piece-work. There was no hourly rate.

DOUG   Deal portin', they used to call it.

LEN D   Working 100% piece-work gives you a certain state of mind and a work ethic, a motivation that most people just don't get. My father, after he'd retired, when he made a cup of tea, he couldn't get out of the habit of trotting from the kitchen to the sitting room because eveything had to be done at the double at the docks.

Tea break. Resting. Sunbathing.

JOHN B   The summer of 1969 was a particularly warm summer. We used to do sunbathing on the roof at lunchtime. it was wonderful sittin' by the river. You know the '*Dock* *o' the Bay,'* Otis Redding? That was bein' played a lot, so I – every time I hear that record, I always think of Hay's Wharf.

There's no comparison, the tea I used to get there to tea bags, it was, it was, er, orange pecan was my favourite tea. My mum always made me sandwiches. Ham. Egg and tomato, yeah, cheese, yeah, yeah, bit of nice good bread.

Sounds of Dock of the Bay as a young chorus enter.

CHORUS   If I were to do it all again, would it be this?

Is this the best I can be?

What choices are there?

Who is it for?

I'll have kids to feed.

I'll have bills to pay.

You dream when you're young, don't you?

LEN D   Solidarity absolutely. We all tended to stick together. It was a family atmosphere in that sense but like all families they occasionally fell out.

Someone pinches his sandwich. Ship's horn. Back to work.

Enter the secretaries, telephonists and clerical assistants. Paper is strewn then filed.

DOROTHY   It was a wonderful place to work. I couldn't have been happier or luckier.

IRENE   Lots of girls, in the offices, yeah.

ANON 2   Plug, you know like the plug, it was like a plug when you put through a call.

IRENE   We used to do all their wages. It was lovely.

DOROTHY   What a lovely job I had. What a lovely place to work.

HEATHER   I had that repetitive strain injury. It's manual and it's the amount of force you've got to do.

BRENDA   He's a very powerful man physically, as well as mentally and he interviewed me and he said 'Well I'd like you to do some typing,' I said 'Yes fine', 'What do you charge?' I said 'Well I either charge by the hour if it's a long job, or by the page if it's short,' so we sorted that out and to this day I can remember him, I'm standing up, he didn't bother asking me to sit down, and I'm standing up and he's walking round looking at me from all angles! *(Laughing)* And he must have thought what the hell have I got here, who's this, curious old-fashioned woman who's appeared from Bermondsey! *(Laughs)* The other end of Rotherhithe tunnel, he's at one end, I'm at the other. I came home, typed it on my beautiful Adler type-writer. He was very impressed.

Dorothy's boss enters She combs his hair and wipes dirt off his face.

DOROTHY My first job was with an assistant to a salesman, and he was a very rich young man, I think he was a relation of Desmond Molins that owned the company. He was very naïve as well, he was difficult to work with, but I was more like his mum than his secretary.

IRENE From typing I wanted to do something different, 'cos typing's boring. I like handling money. So they sent me to the wages office. The people used to come in, they used to put cards in, and their hours and we used to do it on a comptometer. You'd work it like this, you'd work it out and it would come at the bottom. But I just loved it. I loved going to work. You start at the bottom and you work yourself up, you do different jobs and that's what the interesting part about it.

HELEN Of course, when I got married I had to leave because they didn't employ married women. I had two RSA certificates. My typing speed was um, oh God, I don't want to brag about it. The shorthand was 100 wpm and the typing was 70. Then I had my son so that put the... So that was that.

The typists leave – singing:

Oh, have you heard the news, me Johnny,
One more day,
We're homeward bound tomorrow,
One more day,

> Only one more day, me Johnny,
> One more day,
> Oh, rock and roll me over,
> One more day,
> Don't you hear the old man growlin.'

JUNE   It was a thing we accepted. Well I did, I don't know about Joan. I mean I always expected a man to get more money than me. Because, as we used to say, they– they're married, they got children and things like...

JOAN   Oh yeah, it was the done thing.

Chorus of women peeling potatoes. A bucket of potatoes is strewn. Potatoes are collected. Saucepans given. Men come home. They sit. Pans are beaten.

MARY   Yeah, we had bills to pay. We used to share our money anyway. We never had any child benefits or anything like that, no, just had his work money coming in that's all. And when they were on strike, had nothing coming in, and what we saved we were dipping into, and my sister-in-law used to fetch us a load of vegetables. But course' he died in 74 when the two youngsters were 11 and 13 so he never really saw them go out to work. The eldest one we got em, he got an apprenticeship in the print. My Kenny he went to work oh, he was a teacher.

David C's workshop again.

DAVID C   When you were working on the shoemaking, you're working, you actually moulding and sewing on your knees because you're using two arms, because sewing is this action, you know. It's a two-ended... you're sewing from the middle of your thread, or your cord, or whatever it is.

A movement section of threading.

And you sew, not like the machine does it, which is a lock stitch. It's not the same, this way it actually goes backwards and forwards through the material and it holds much better. And it's also waxed with a very sticky wax – that when you pull it through it melts. Friction will melt the wax. When you stop pulling it, it will dry and then you can't move it. You have to, once you pull it, you got to pull it all the way and tight. Because in that time the wax, because you had the wax and you had to make... the threads are made of say seven strands of hemp, or nine strands of hemp. And you have to actually make this yourself. Because you make it one length, tapered at the end, you actually used bristles, boar's bristle. And you had to actually twist it onto the tread, twist it with the wax onto the thread, the cord, and then you sewed with that.

Music fades to blustering wind. High up on a crane.

JOHN T   We used to have to go out repair or look after the main machinery for the actual crane itself. The man I was working with would lower the jib, so we'd be going down and the ball would go out and then he'd bring it back up and the ball would come up and when it came I gotta grab it. *(Claps)* I often wondered, you know, if you put your hand in the wrong place you'd have gone clap you'd have smashed it.

DAVE F   The crane was lifting some metal girders, for the guys in the lift shaft, the lift runs up and down and, um, cable snapped, and these straight rails came down and hit the ground. From about, must have been thirty floors up then. When the metal hit the ground it just buckled, it was dead straight to start with as it went up but when it came down and hit the floor it was all buckled, but nobody was injured luckily, and just no one in the way at the time.

JUNE   There wasn't any health and safety.

DOUG   There might be health but there wasn't safety.

STEVE   I remember one of the first things I did as a factory inspector was to go with the inspector that was training me to help him investigate this accident where a person had got caught on the stock bar of a lathe, and been turned round and round, been dragged off his feet by the force, gone round and round and round and broke various bones in his body. And it was very serious. It was an absolute standard thing that you should fence the stock bar of the lathe, and that hadn't. And this chap had got very badly injured. When I say it's less than two hundred people being killed, it is less than two hundred people killed, but it is still around two hundred people being killed as a result of work activity.

JOHN B   If you was feeling you were unhappy with something, if you didn't complain then they wouldn't do anything about it and it depended on how many of you did complain, or-and-and how forceful in your complaint, whether they ignored you-or-or not.

BERT   Oh yeah, one of my mates, used to live in my street, they dropped a car or somethin' on top of him. Out of the crane y'know, he was takin' it out the ship, y'know on the hooks and all that lark and it just let go of it and it went down and killed him outright.

A funeral. An undertaker speaks to audience.

BARRY   If you listen you will learn as much as they will learn. When someone first comes in I try to get them comfortable and not to talk about it to begin with. Can I get you something? Can I get you some tea? You've probably been out all day. Let's talk about your day and the difficulties you've had. I want you to be treated as a name and not a number 'cos you've probably been at the hospital with ten other families or twenty other families waiting to be seen in rotation. This should be the first time you've sat in a comfortable environment and you relax and you talk to a family as life goes on about you. Because life and death are the same factor, they are just different moments within them.

The funeral dissolves. Enter a drunken cat.

JOHN B　　There was this, er, big old ginger tomcat, used to prowl around Mark Brown's Wharf and St Olave's! It was a huge thing, a huge big head, all scarred, half his ear missing, but a really big old cat. And there'd be all these wine barrels, and there'd be a little tray underneath, where the tap would be on so they could take samples, but it would drip And that cat used to go around and drink the drips. And you'd see 'm up there he would, staggerin' from side to side. Drunk! Drunken old tom cat! And e' was good at killin' rats as well, but he wandered onto The Baltic Sun once, to sleep it off. And it ended up in Poland!

CHORUS　　A million million man hours moan

Metals wrought,

Cranes strain,

The foundaries ablaze with coal and ore.

Streams of men and women
Memoranda, computations,
Statistical analysis of the day to
day and year to year.
Boardrooms, tea rooms
Back rooms, new brooms,
Commodities converted and
exchanges fair and square
A seething river of things and lives
and loss and profit.
And then stock still
They catch their breath
And examine their time and place.
What is the meaning of my hours?
What is this space inside myself?
I've got kids to feed.
I've got bills to pay.
You dream when you're young,
don't you?

A spirit of slightly hysterical pleasure-seeking takes possession of everyone. Some sneaky drinking.

DAVE F   I worked for Chelsure Brothers in Tooley Street, on the wine bottling line, underneath the arches. And there was occasion when you took a sneaky drink out of the bottle. Everyone was sneaking behind the bottling line.

JOHN T   Wines and spirits were in the bond, what they call the bond which was run by the customs – you couldn't get in and you couldn't get out without being checked, but while you were in there...

ANON 2   You'd go out Friday lunchtime for a drink, shouldn't be drinking but we used to have a drink at lunch. And sausages and chips it's just in the pubs. And we'd go out Friday night and Saturday night.

The trocadero cinema. A bit of hanky panky on the back row.

IRENE   We went to go pictures with it – and you'd get fish and chips for sixpence. And I remember the first boy came, he took me to the pictures and when I come back you know, I said, the girls said to me how'd you get on so I said 'Oooh he took up in the one and nines' which was posh then– 'cos there was a big cinema at Elephant and Castle, the Trocadero.

The back row.

SPEED   That's why they used to call me "Speed". Cos' the more I worked the more money I got and and... So you know I could go to the pictures and I could buy tights. No, not tights, stockings. Fine ones.

SPEED   Somebody said to me the other week 'Would you have changed your life?' and I said 'Would I do anything different?' And I said 'No,' and she was amazed, well, well if my life meant changing my late husband, ooh I wouldn't he was a love, love of my life.

CHORUS　And out in the further darkness
of the Quays by night.
Helping themselves to their heart's desire.
Men breaking in to cargo.

PAT D　There was a guy called Diesel. And I was working with him on the first ship I worked on called the John Hunter. I said 'Why do they call this bloke Diesel?' I said to one of them and he said 'You'll find out.' He actually cut the seal which was put on by the customs, which, that's – terrible trouble, and he would creep into the cargo hold, and you could hear him saying 'These'll do for the missus! 'Diesel' do for the kids! 'Diesel' do for me!' Everybody knew he did it. Even the police knew he did it!

Men hide the loot down their trousers.

JUNE　The only ones that got perks was the ones that nicked it! 'Specially among dockers! On the boats, they'd come with, erm, legs of lamb down their trousers, tied round and walk out.

BERT　You see that clock? That come out the dock. It was one of my uncles that give me that.

CHORUS　Bosses ceased to be your betters.
They ceased to be visible.

They were faceless.

They were global.

Decisions were made, but they didn't have to look you in the eye.

JOHN T   There was always a fight on, you was always going to go out on strike. The Electrical Trade Union which was absolutely communist, but not in a way of radical, there was no fighting or anything – they just wanted, the communists at the time wanted fair shares for everybody – which sounded alright to me. Used to be about once a month and they used to be held over a pub, down in Bermondsey – ah, it was the Blue Anchor.

LEN H   Because there was a very, very bad feelin' toward dock employers. In the 1889 dock strike they come out for a guaranteed six pence an hour, they won it after a long period but then, within a month or so, it was taken away from then again. It's the same in the General Strike, when the General Strike was on in 19, well 1929.

LEN H   Where I worked at Bellamy's Wharf there was two men there, Friday night I spoke to him this particular man and I was told, 'What you speak to him for?' 'Oh well, I just–' 'Well don't,' it was, that was a bitter feelin' amongst the older clan 'cause he went to work at the time and so there was still. He was sent to Coventry.

LEN H   When I started in the dock there used to be 12 men workin' on the ship, when I was at Tilbury there was only 6 men down the 'ole, everythin' was palletisation and containerisation. Where the rats went, it was in the water – where they went I don't know *(Laughs)* but they musta gone somewhere.

Men in dinner jackets walk through, smoking cigarettes, wryly surveying the scene. In response a picket line is formed. Police watching. Placards have messages of protest and solidarity. There is a smaller placard to the side that says 'History...?'

CHORUS   I've got kids to feed.

I've got bills to pay.

Who is this for?

Who is this for?

The men in dinner jackets, confident in themselves, smile and walk away.

PAT K   Everything was a bit gloomy to be honest in the 1970s. The docks were closing down, so there was a feeling of decay like the place was, going down. The people were still great, but the area felt like it was going down.

Picket line turns into a funeral. Hats removed. Coffin carried. The 'History...?' placard is still visible.

LEN H   When Mrs Margaret Thatcher *(Pause)* I came out just before that, but after, but after I just come out she refused to sign the National Dock Labour Board agreement so that gave a lot of the employers *(Pause)* a chance to sack you. Which they did. And there was a big strike at Tilbury then but there was no men there *(Laughs)* the convoys sacked 'em all, waved them bye-bye.

Coffin lowered into the ground.

BARRY   The first thing to remember is that the body is sacred. That's where we start. How we remove you, the vehicle we put you in. The vehicle they're moved in is very important. It's not the end of their life, its an extension of the journey. So I like people to be in their own clothes. I'm very fussy about that. The carrying of the person reflects straight back to how sacred that is. Measuring people up correctly to be in the right place. Putting people in the right coffin. We have bells that will ring and chime as we leave. It has good balance to it.

Coffin. Sound of the river. Gulls. Silence. Empty stage.

A child wearing a card Margaret Thatcher mask plays hopscotch. She is joined by other world leaders in masks.

Silence.

The London Stock Exchange pre-computerisation.
Dealers shouting at each other to sell and buy.

VANESSA   I've always been a bit not pushy about
moving on really, I need someone to
give me a push and they said 'Oh they're
short in the dealing room, would you
like to just go there for six months, and
see how you get on?' And I thought I
don't fancy doing that because it was all
like open outcry you know, you have to
shout across the room, you know:

YOUNG VANESSA 'How do you sell a million Belgian
francs?'

VANESSA   and everybody looking at me, but I
thought I'll give it a go. I loved it, I loved
it yeah.

YOUNG VANESSA When I was doing Canadian dollars
well say I want to buy 500,000 Canadian
dollars, you know, how, what rate will
you sell them to me at – and then you
talked, you'd have lines to brokers and
you'd say 'What's your price?' So you
would um you would quote a price that
you could cover yourself and make a
small margin.

VANESSA   There was shouting,

YOUNG VANESSA There'd be shouting

BOTH   You had to shout, you'd shout across the
room to people.

VANESSA   I was happy where I was and um, the
potential for higher pay and promotion.

YOUNG VANESSA It became it gradually became harder, I'd say it became harder and harder – there was a kind of, it must of been in the late 80s, where people were coming in and once we merged with Lloyds Bank International they were taking people on and we had people who were from Oxford and Cambridge with first class and 2:1s in computer science. But, er, I had the advantage of experience, there was this experience against the new people coming in, but it got very fast, you had to have really, really sharp mind and you started looking at um, what would you call it, it was called, the, you were looking at opportunities to trade between different, different sorts of products and that, it wasn't just, it was no longer straight. I left in 1999 and took early retirement.

CHORUS The average daily turnover of the currency market is in excess of $4 trillion dollars. There are 400,000 grains in a handful of sand. There are only 300 billion stars in the Milky Way.

Sand is poured from a wheelbarrow. The River Thames is etched into the sand. Canary Wharf is constructed from packets of biscuits.

IRENE They wanted to teach me computers, I said, 'No, I don't want to learn that because you're going to get rid of me anyway.' I was 58. We used to have to do our brain. The finest thing going your brain, it's the finest thing going – you have to use it.

BRENDA   I didn't use the computer till about 2003. I was sort of reluctant, but now I see what a great help it is. But it did take me a bit of time to sort of come round to it.

JOHN B   Newspapers would say that, they brought this on their selves, and docks are closing 'cause the dockers wanted too much money. Absolute rubbish of course. It was, cuz of containerisation was comin' and Hay's Wharf wanted to flog the land, the land was worth more money than what they could make runnin' the docks.

DAVE F   Upmarket people. You know, I don't know whether you call 'em yuppies or what – but they had a better living than I had if you know what I mean – they had better jobs than I had. We wanna live in London, we wanna live by the river… We want a nice river view. Council was bumping up the rents to equal the rent of the new places. Working class people couldn't really keep on finding the money to pay more.

The men in dinner jackets return. The cast illustrate the following with boxes.

MEN   Richard Sennett identified five types of human exchange:

Altruism where you give with no desire for reward:

Win-win – an exchange that benefits all the participants:

Differentiating exchange – a negotiation that respects difference, to minimise competition for resources or territory:

Zero-sum – where one's gain is another's loss. However, the loser is left with enough to carry on in the zero sum game in the hope of winning another time.

And winner-takes-all – where the predator takes everything and the loser is destroyed:

The biscuit factory. Chorus weave in between the present day occupants with microphones and video cameras.

CHORUS In 1999 the Biscuit Factory was reopened as part of Tower Bridge Business Complex; tastefully converted to suit media-style businesses seeking a central London location"

ALI I've got the cafe.

MARK I own the Vibe Gallery.

FRED I run the climbing wall.

IKE I do video productions, TV adverts. Stuff like that.

DAVE And I'm the caretaker.

ALI I'm usually up at five in the morning.

IKE I finish about 3am.

ALI	Full English Breakfasts. A lot of sandwich mixes.
IKE	I'm also a camera man, lighting engineer, sound engineer, editing...
FRED	Best thing? When you get a new group of people come in that have never done it before and they get hooked.
DAVE	I spend a lot of time in the car park giving people directions.
MARK	Cabarets, art installations, performance art...
FRED	At about four o'clock or so I have a climb myself.
MARK	Music evenings...
DAVE	We've got plenty of cameras- on-site, so if somebody wanted to check up on you, they could. I like to come in and do a day's work.
ALI	I always wanted to be a boxer... I'm 50 now. Not long to retire.

Elders back in their interview chairs being interviewed.

Recorded.

MARY	I've done all the decorating in this. Bedrooms, papered all the bedrooms. I put shelves up. And put mirrors up when they wanted. I've got a drill. I do a lot of crochet. I'm making a doll's outfit for the new baby. I do my own cooking. My son

only comes Thursday for an apple pie, I'm sure he does.

LEN H   When I went into the dock there was somewhere around about 42,000 dockers in London dock system, when I came out there was only 9,000. I vowed I'd come out at 55, I wouldn't work any longer in the dock and I did come out, I be honest with you, I got severance money, but I missed what I had at the beginning, casual, very good friends, mates, very good laughs, silly things sometimes y'know.

DAVE M   I go in every Thursday morning help children with their reading, and I'm so pleased to be there. It is so lovely hearing the children sing.

CHORUS   Photographs in empty halls.
Old time tunes and cups of tea.
There's the grandchildren.
And the pension.
And the time you have spent
Getting things done.

BARRY   When I was a kid and I walked along Tanner Street, all I could smell was the hide, the leather. As I walked up Bermondsey Street there were other smells, because you had where they made mink, which were quite vile smells, then you walked further up and you had the perfume factory. Then you'd get to Pearce Duff's and you had the custard stewing, you know. Then you'd get to the Blue and have Edwards or Spa bakery with that lovely bread smell, then you'd get to where the biscuits were being baked, coconut on a Thursday, Bournville on a Friday, you know. So everything in this area is summed up with smells. There are new smells now. There's the Mogul I can smell, with the lovely spices as you go passed. There is the Turkish bakery at the back of the shop opposite. The smells are still there. The smells are just different. And the people are just different.

DAVID C What you achieve – when you see the person you know, was actually able to walk. The achievement. This is it, because it is an achievement.

CHILD My hands. My ears. My eyes.
My face. My smile. My suffering.
My judgement. My knowledge. My skills.
My strength. My courage. My luck.
My time. My life. My labour.

The end.

London Bubble community activities

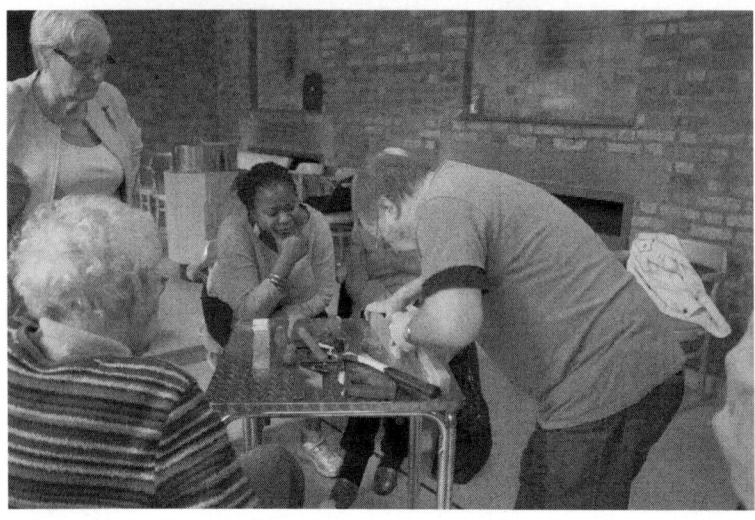

Exploratory workshops: 'If it's a job worth doing' June 2013

From Docks to Desktops roadshow Burgess Park May Fair
May 2013

First scratch performance during Creativity and Wellbeing
June 2013

Shaun, Jean, Deshaye and Joan

Mary Ripper interviewed by Kemi Lofinmakin
December 2012

BLACKBIRDS

by Simon Startin

In the first month of the Blitz alone, 5,730 people were killed and 9,003 seriously injured. By the end of the Blitz in May 1940, just 9 months later, 43,000 people had been killed, half of them in London.

Some of the 'children of the blitz' who survived this are still alive today but when do we ask about their experiences? Who is going to preserve their account, an essential piece of London history which will help us understand the reality of life in the capital during the second World War?

Blackbirds is the story of Londoners who lived through the most extreme conditions of the Blitz and are here to tell the tale, in their own words. Collected by local children and performed by local people it was performed for the first time by the London Bubble Theatre Company.

In an age when we are connected by global networks, but don't know our neighbours, *Blackbirds* tells of a time when bombs fell daily in the street and Britain was at its bravest.

For history students, students of drama, and anyone else with an interest in period drama and first-hand accounts of WWII. *Blackbirds* is also intended for use in schools and colleges, amateur groups, and youth theatres.

ISBN 978-1-906582-29-6 £8.99

Available from

www.aurorametro.com

Aurora Metro Books

some of our other play collections

NEW PLAYS FOR YOUNG PEOPLE by Charles Way
ISBN 978-0-906582-51-7 £12.99

PLAYS FOR YOUNG PEOPLE by Charles Way
ISBN 978-0-953675-71-5 £9.95

THE CLASSIC FAIRYTALES Retold for the Stage by Charles Way
ISBN 978-0-954233-00-6 £11.50

THE CLASSIC FAIRY TALES 2 Retold for the Stage by Charles Way
ISBN 978-0-955156-67-0 £11.99

THE DUTIFUL DAUGHTER by Charles Way
ISBN 978-0-954691-26-4 £7.99

A SPELL OF COLD WEATHER by Charles Way
ISBN 978-0-954233-08-2 £7.99

MERLIN AND THE CAVE OF DREAMS by Charles Way
ISBN 978-0-955156-60-1 £7.99

PLAYS FOR YOUTH THEATRES AND LARGE CASTS by Neil Duffield
ISBN 978-1-906582-06-7 £12.99

THEATRE CENTRE: Plays for Young People selected and introduced
by Rosamunde Hutt
ISBN 978-0-954233-05-1 £12.99

NEW SOUTH AFRICAN PLAYS ed. Charles J. Fourie
ISBN 978-0-954233-01-3 £11.99

BLACK AND ASIAN PLAYS Anthology introduced by Afia Nkrumah
ISBN 978-0-953675-74-6 £12.99

BALKAN PLOTS: New Plays from Central and Eastern Europe ed.
Cheryl Robson
ISBN 978-0-953675-73-9 £9.95

www.aurorametro.com